HAIRCUTS OF HACKNEY

*A visual encylopaedia of
East London hair*

DANIEL FROST

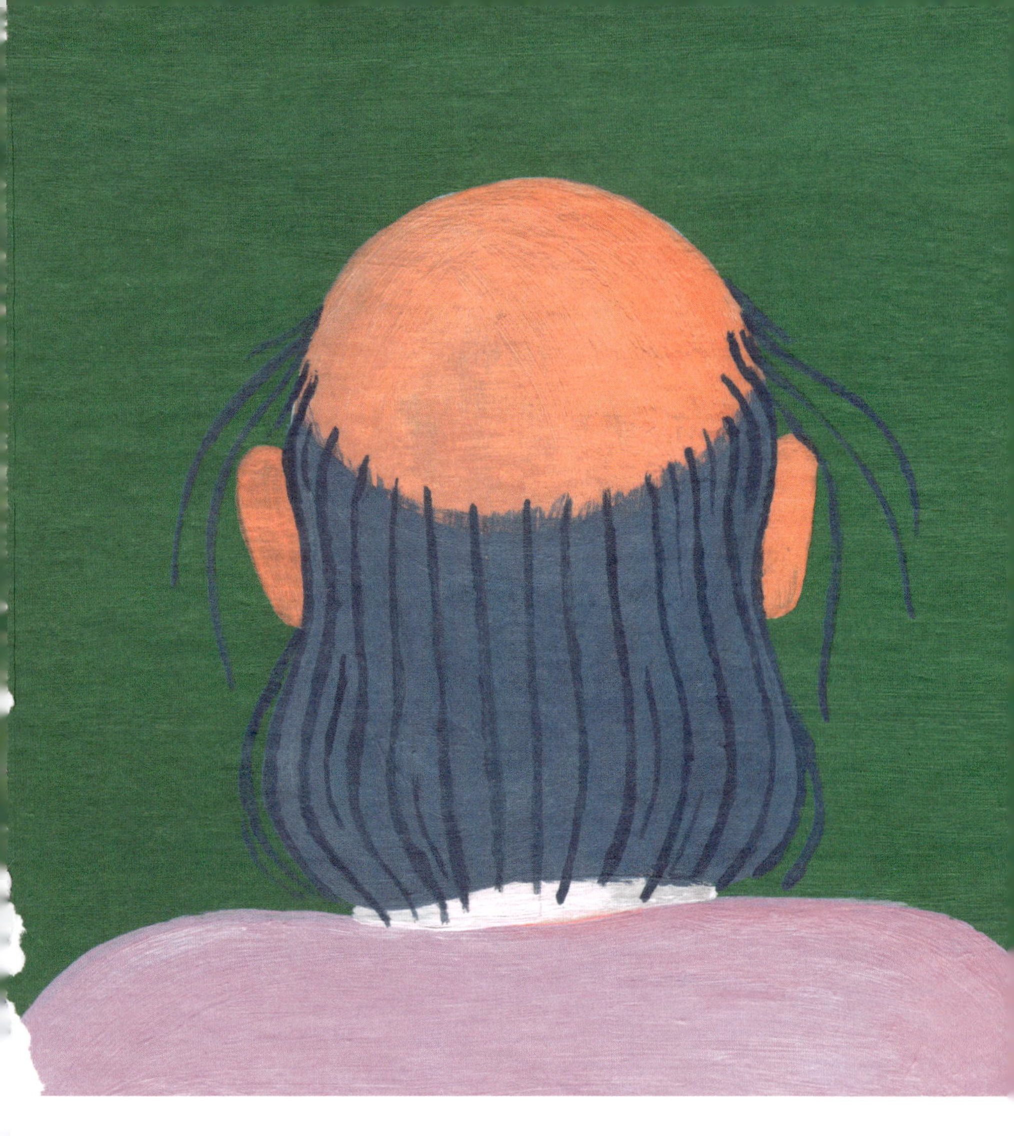

Skullet

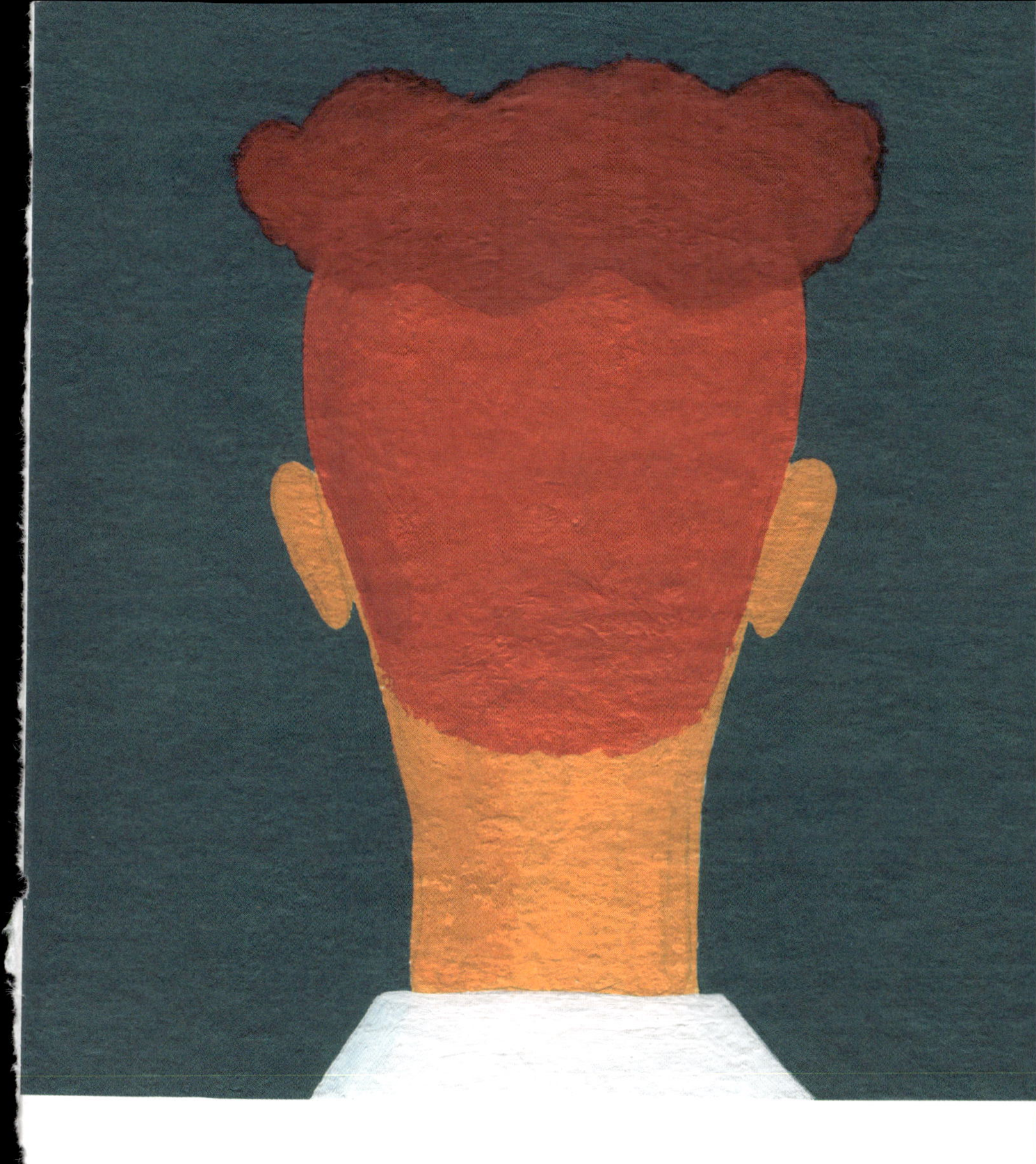

Moptop

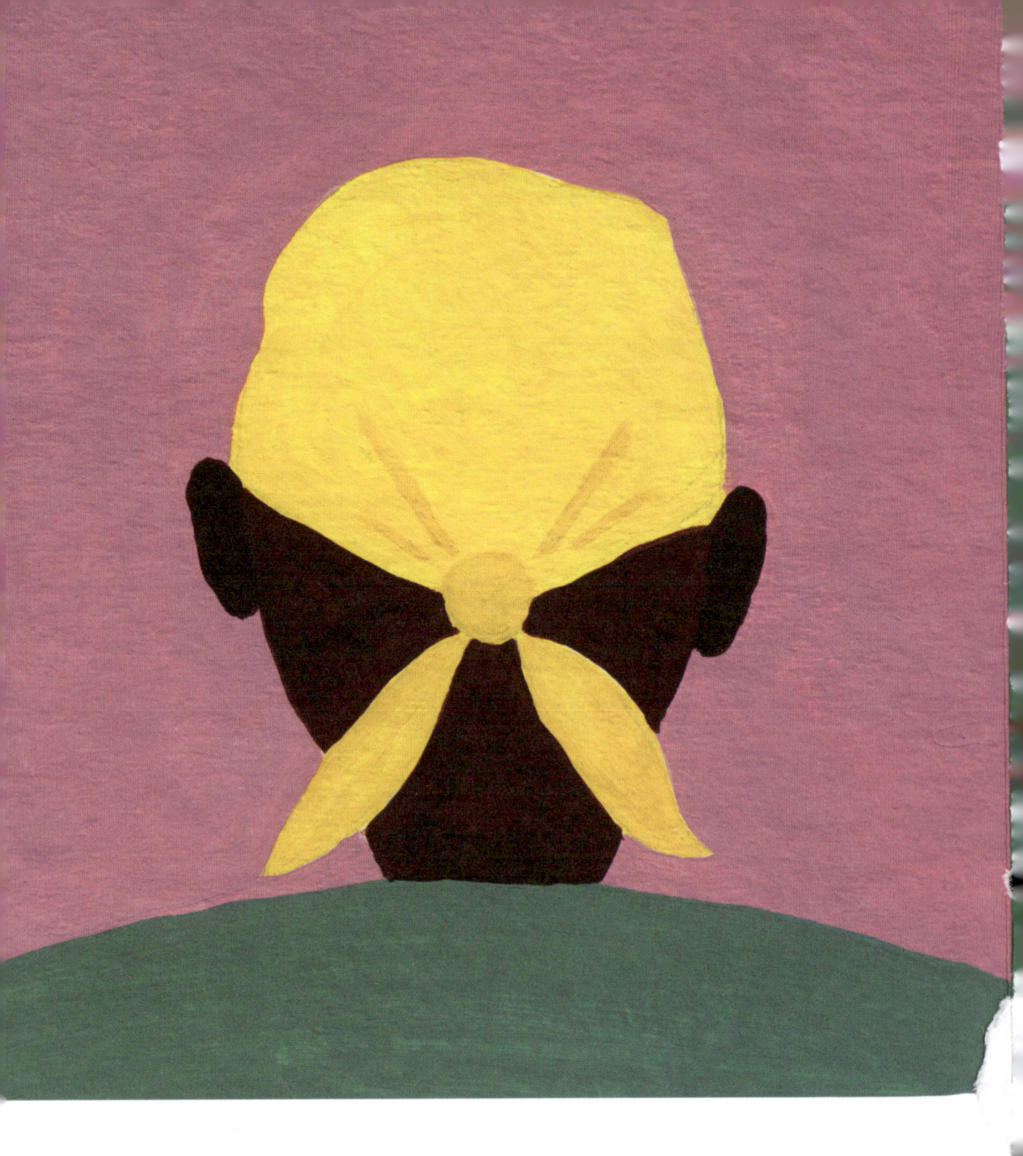

Do-rag

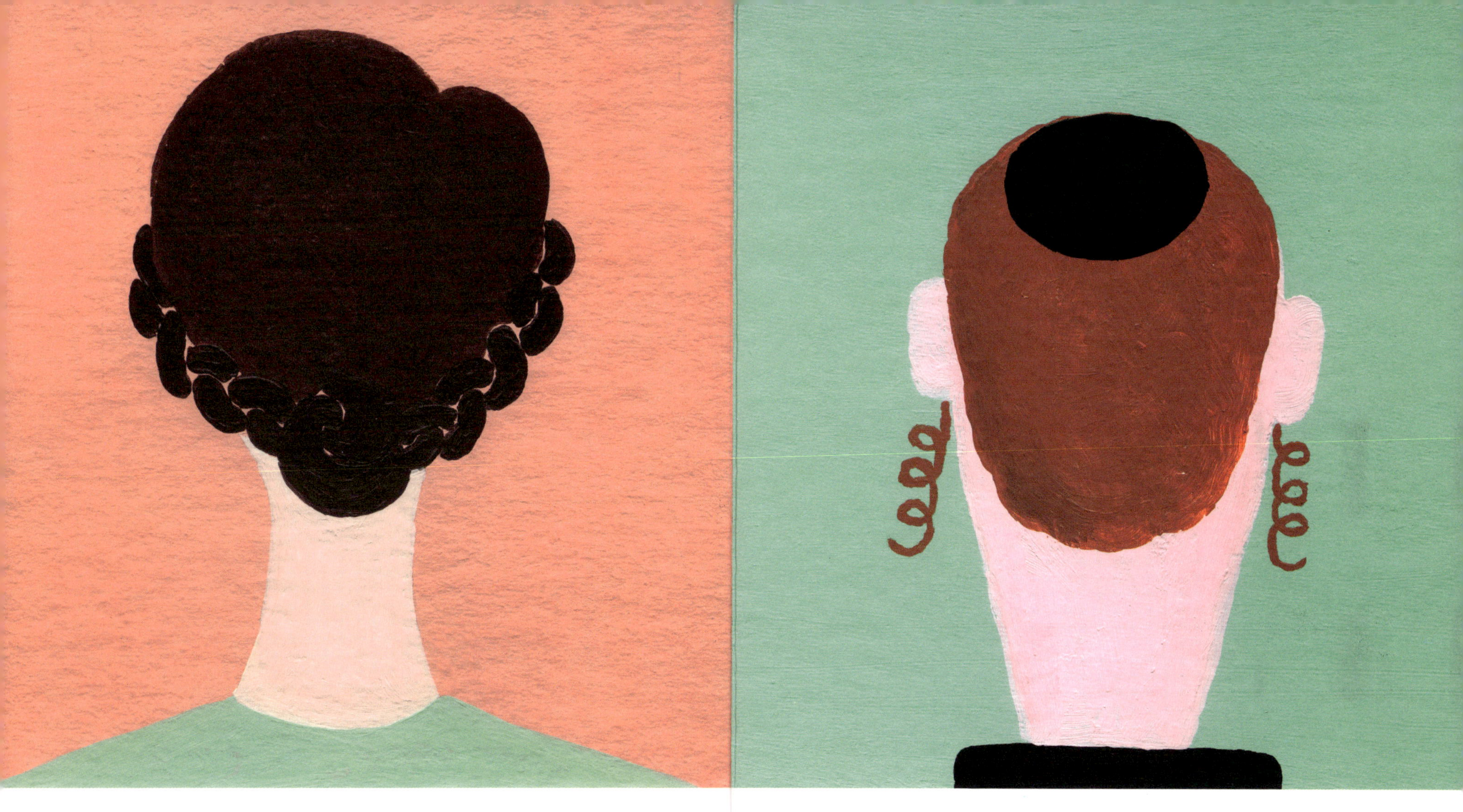

Pretzel

Orthodox Locks

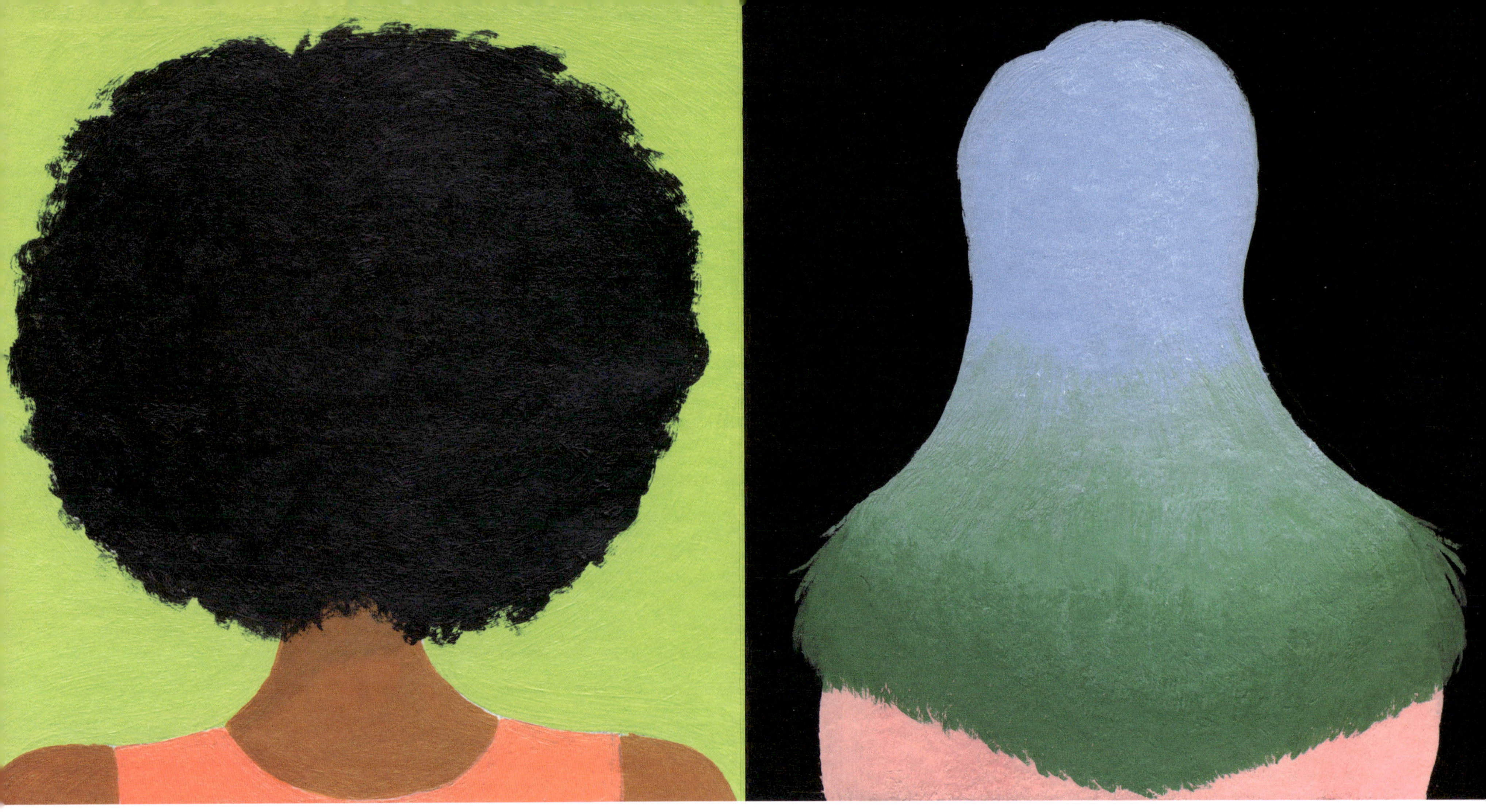

Fro   Dalston Two-tone

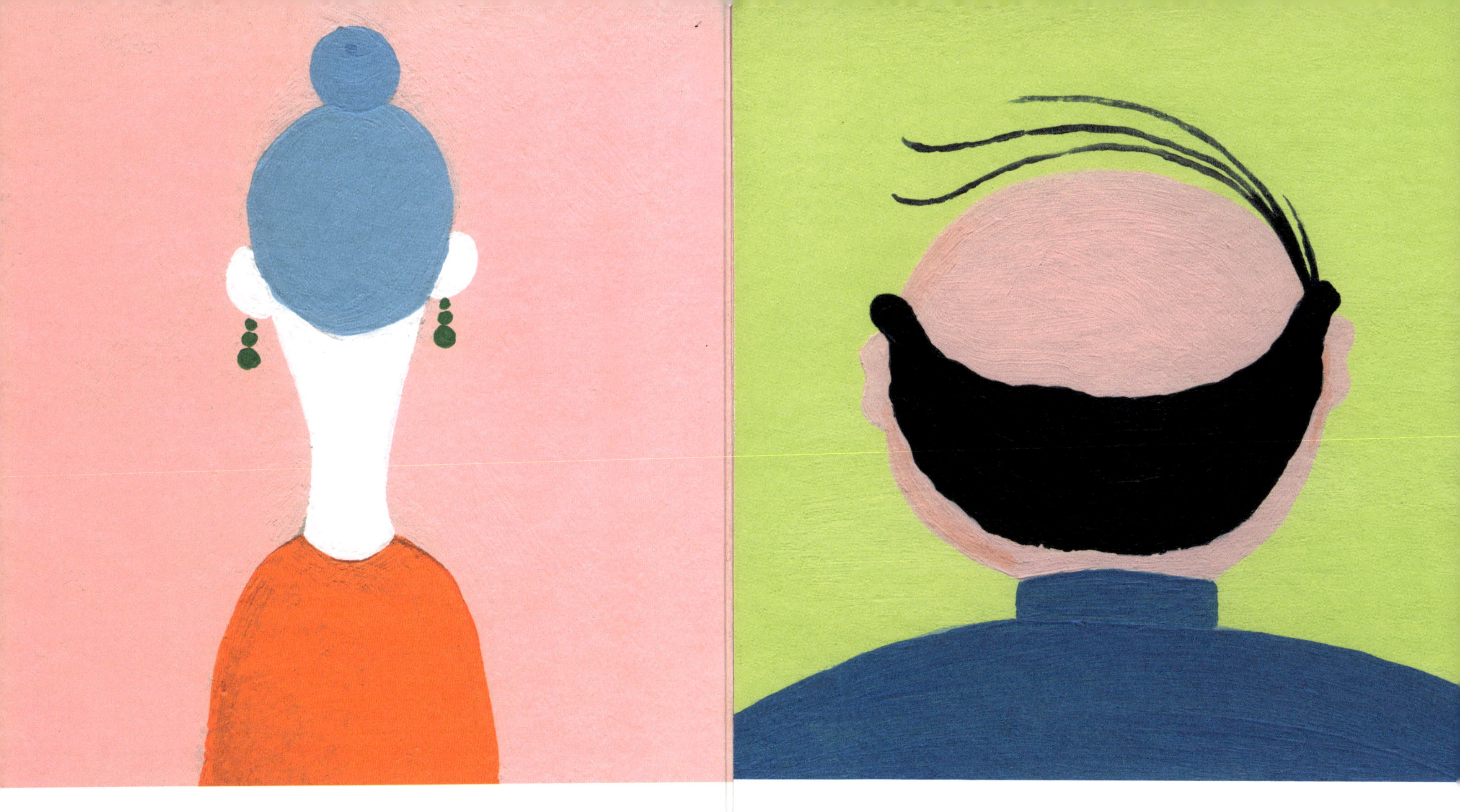

Mrs Peacock

Comb-over

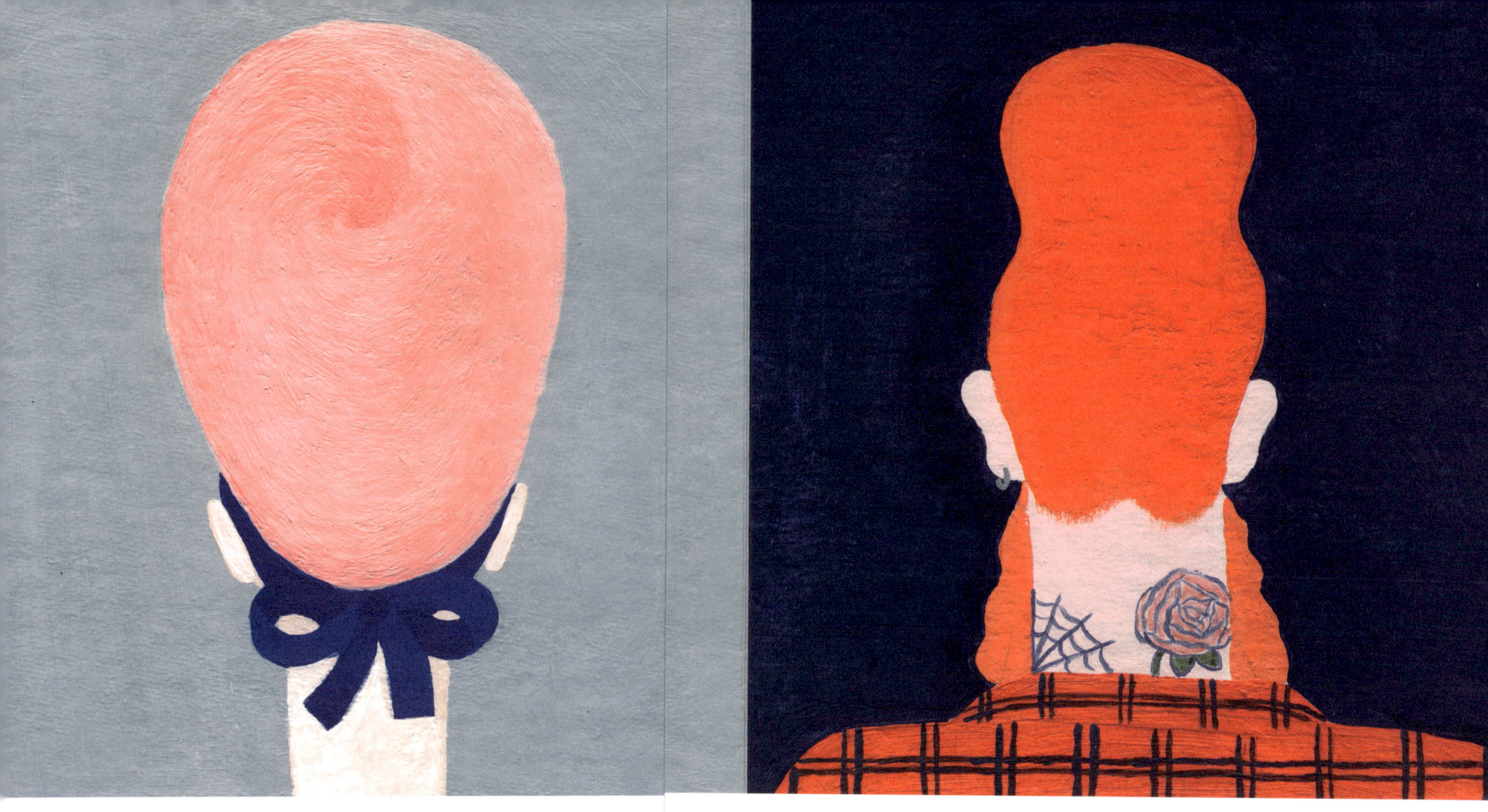

Beehive

Beardway Market

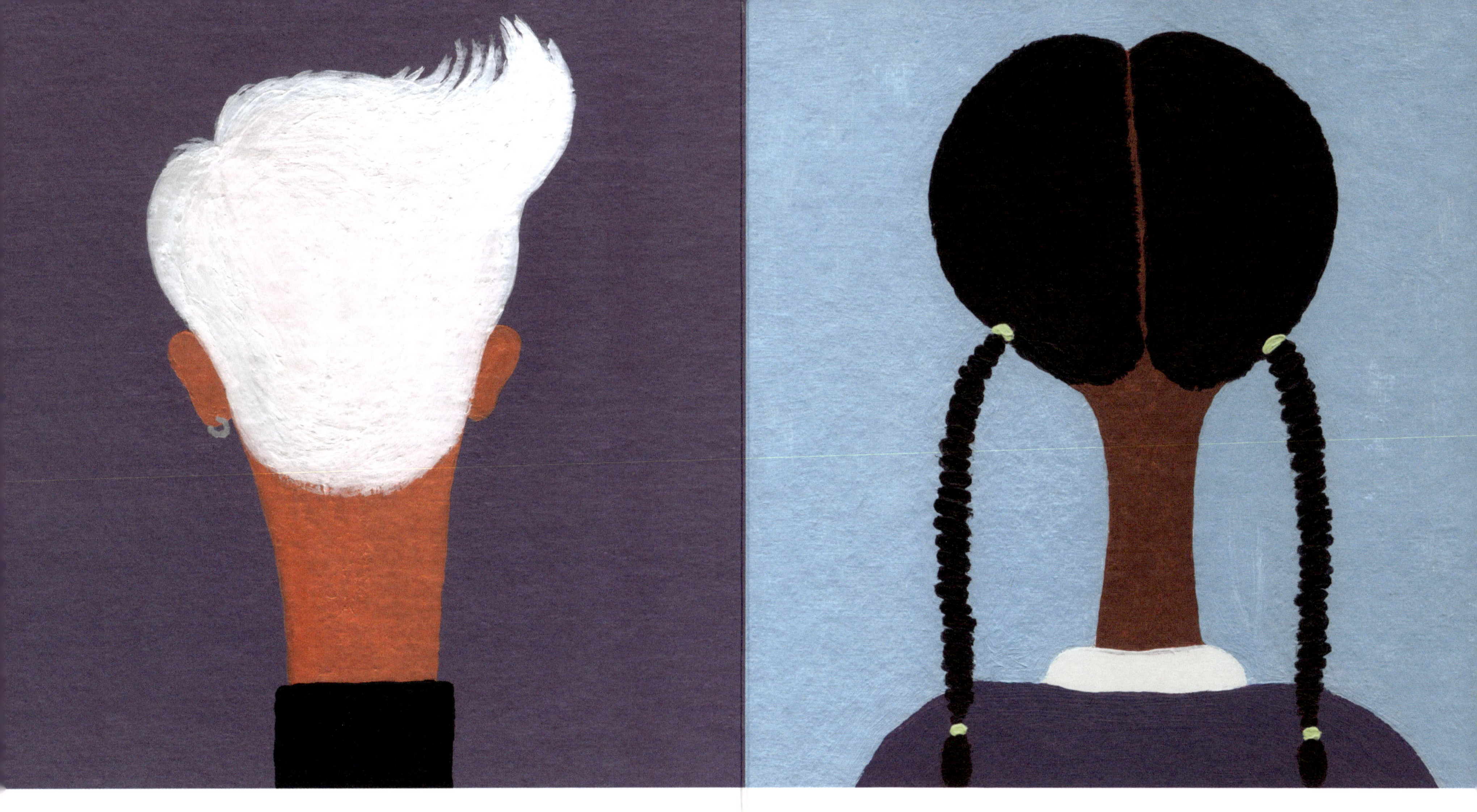

Queensbridge Quiff

Pigtails

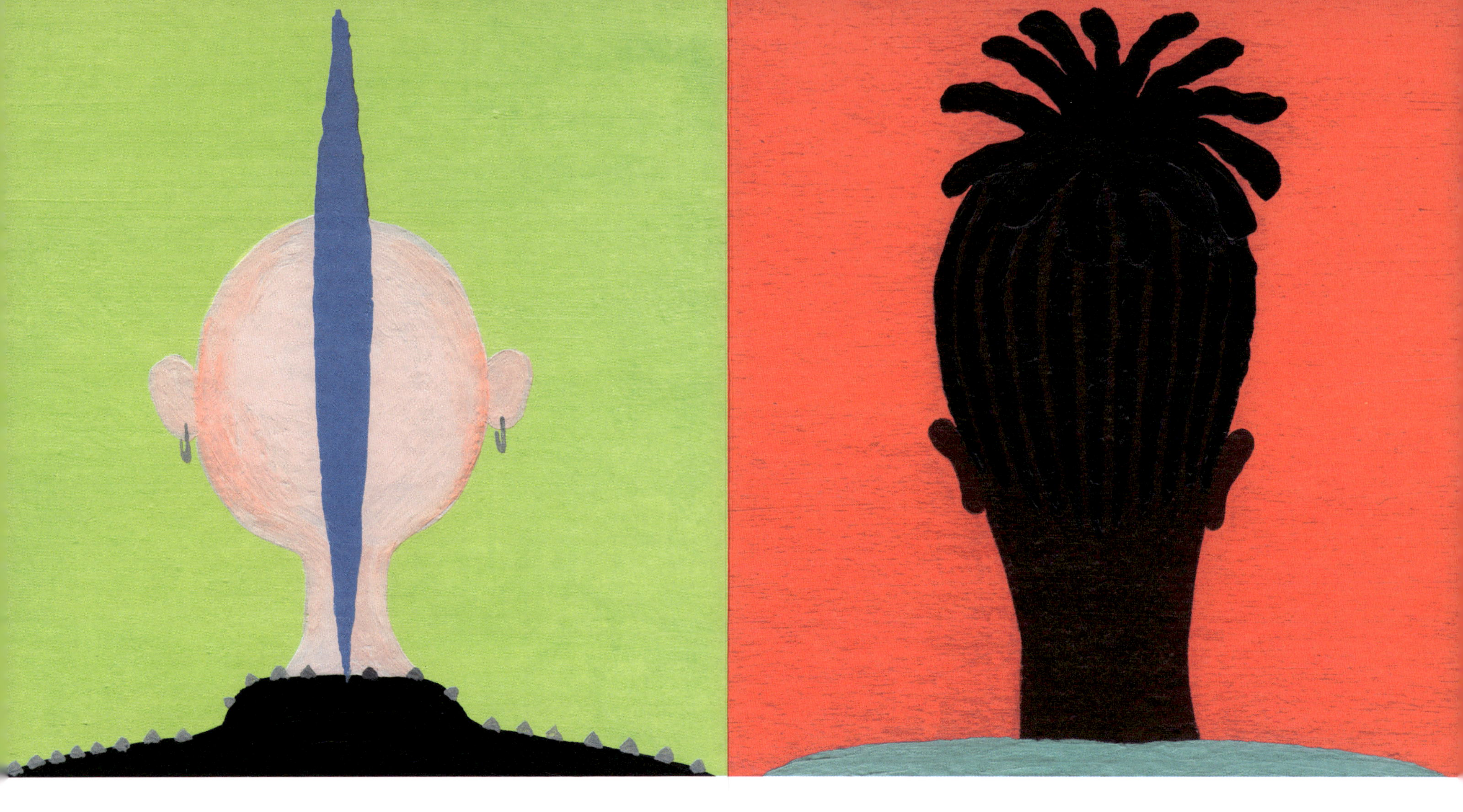

Bowhawk

Ridley Rows

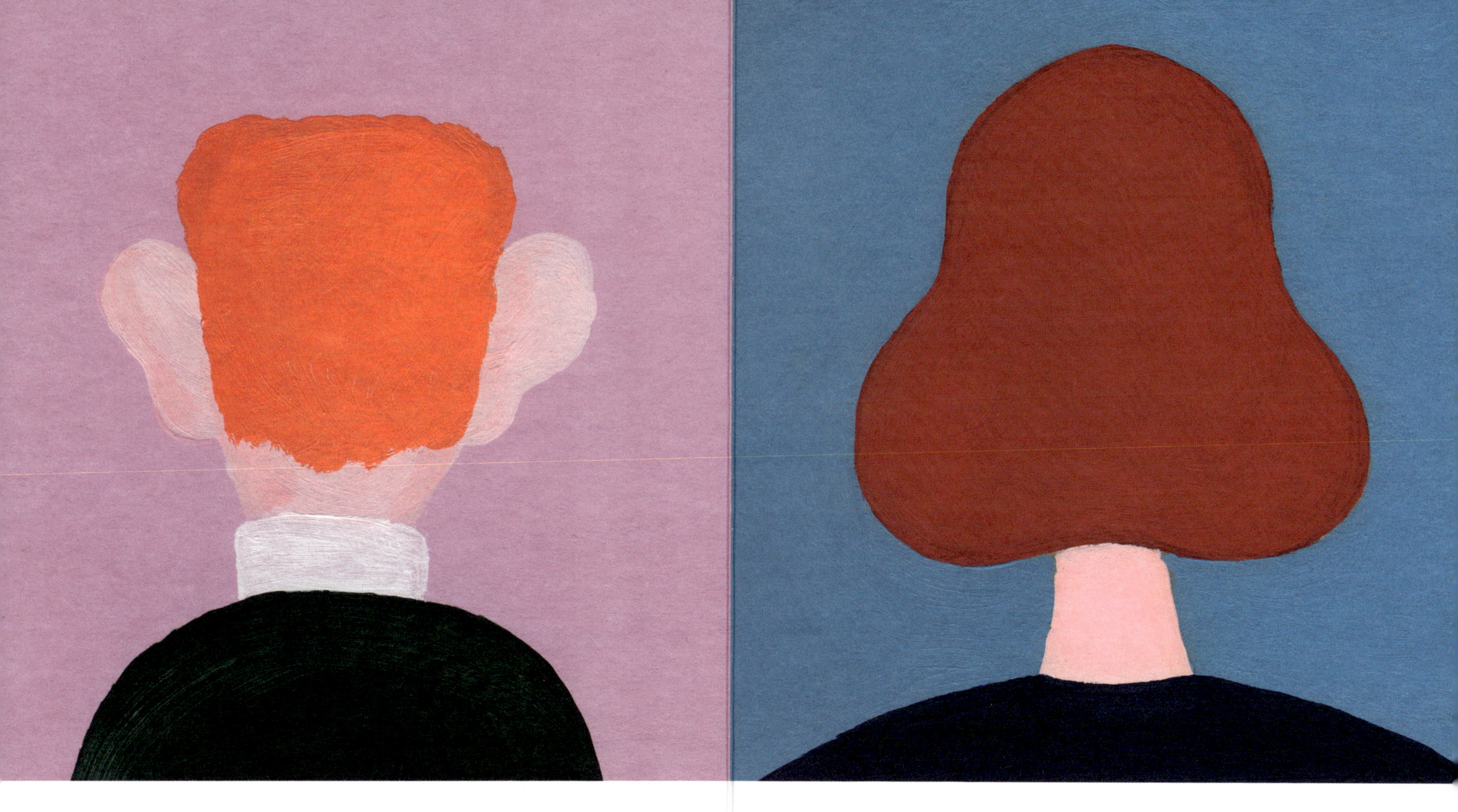

Wing Nut

Pageboy

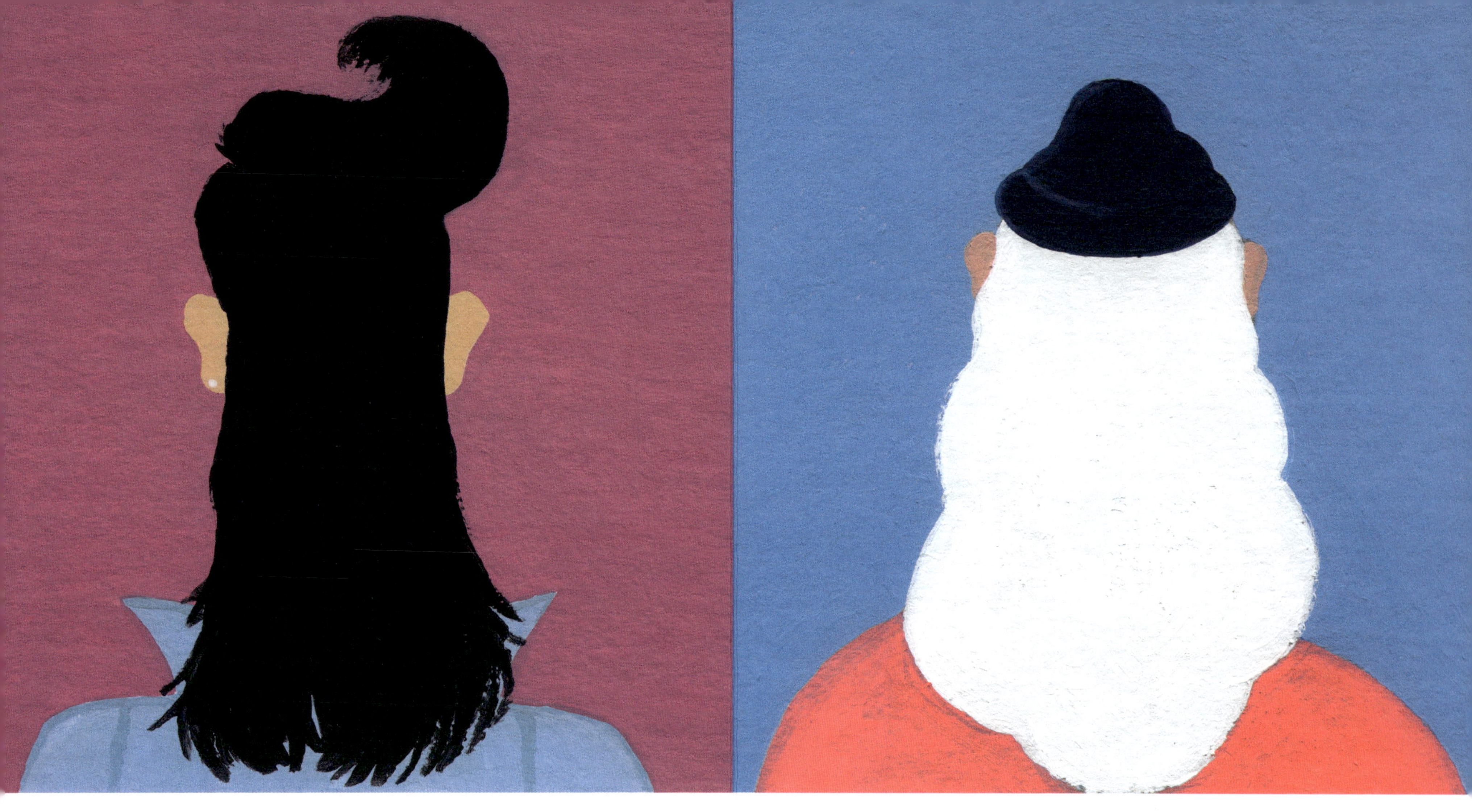

Well Street Waterfall

Arnold Circus

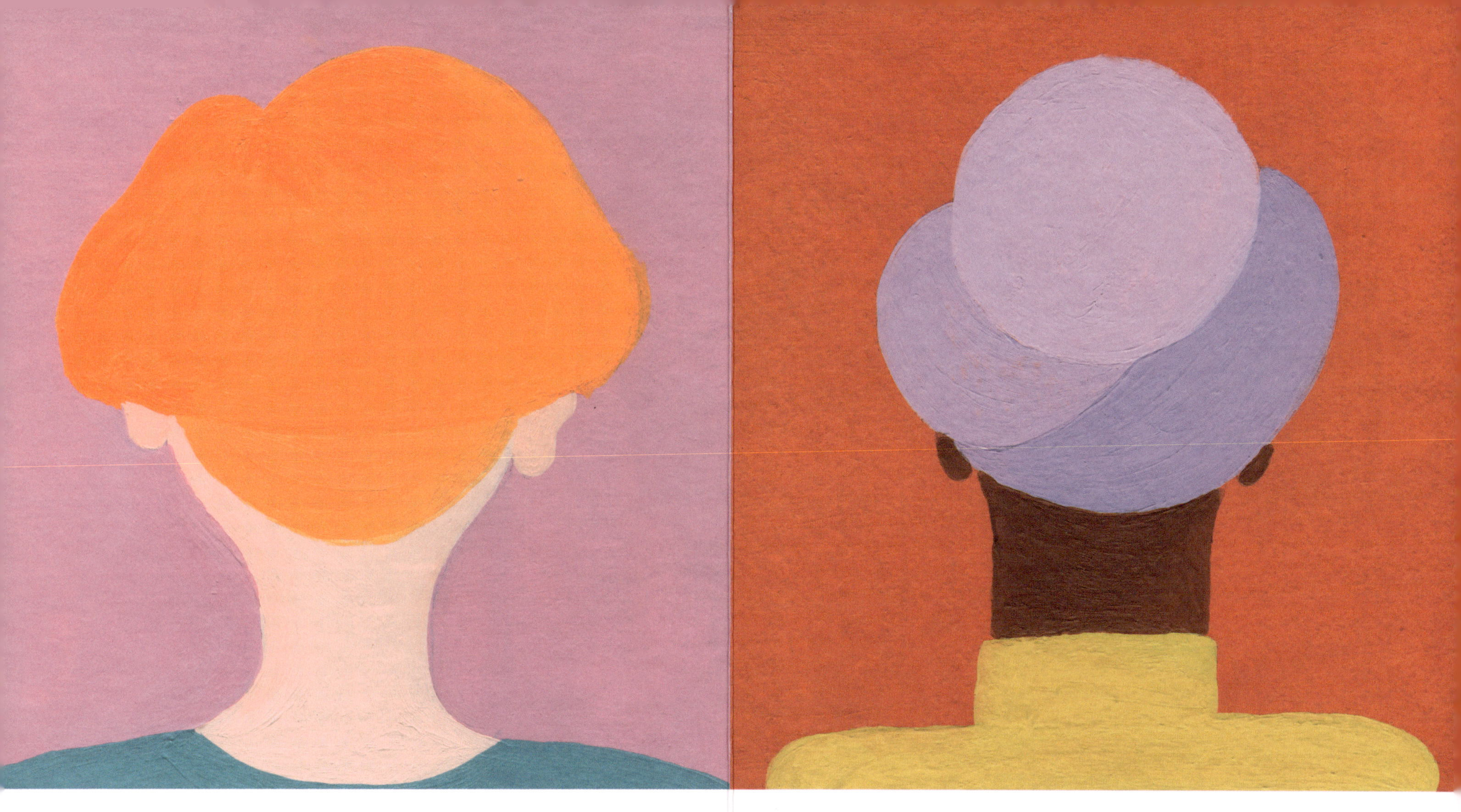

Kingsland Basin

Clapton Wrap

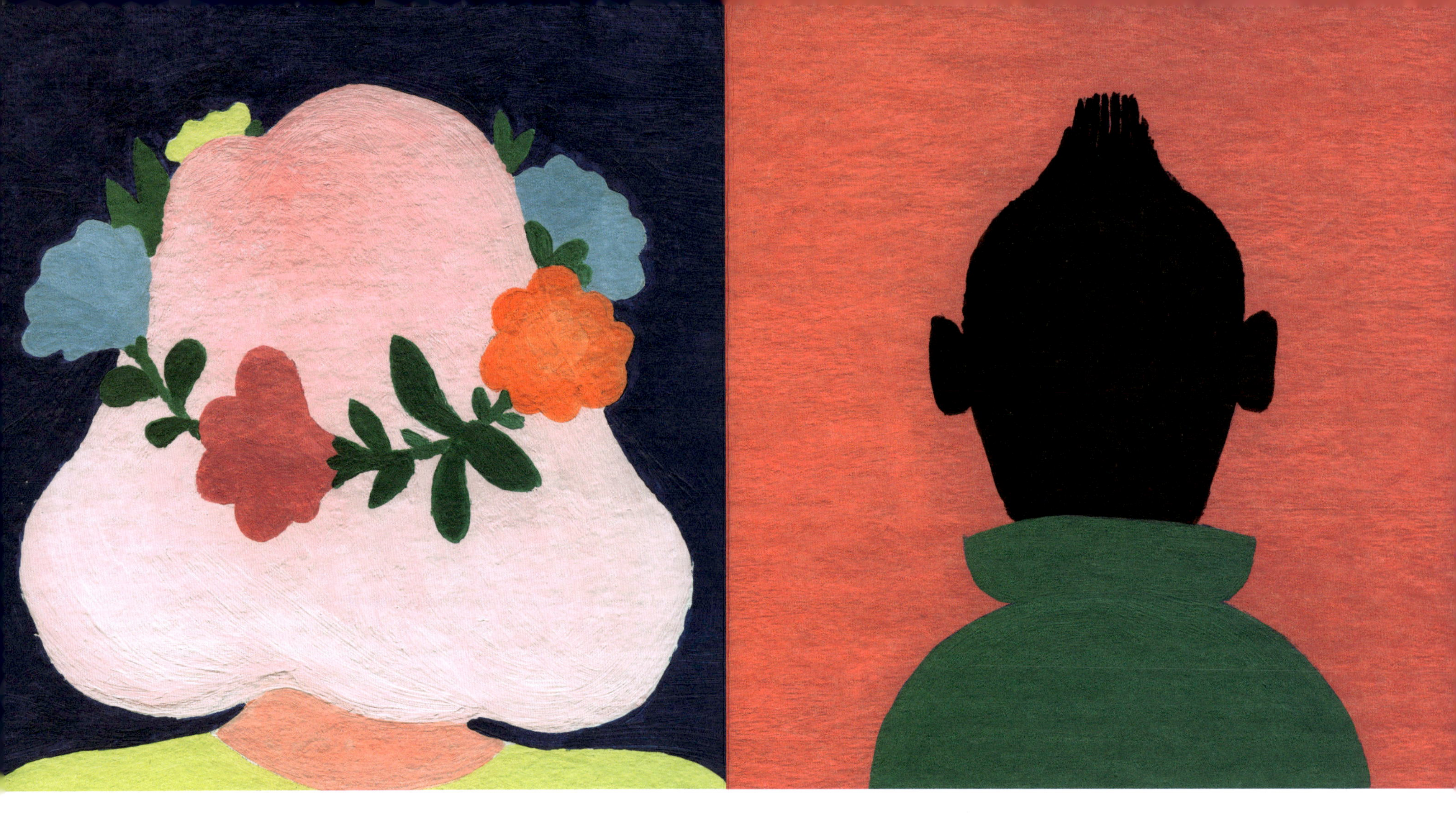

London Fields   Hoxton Fin

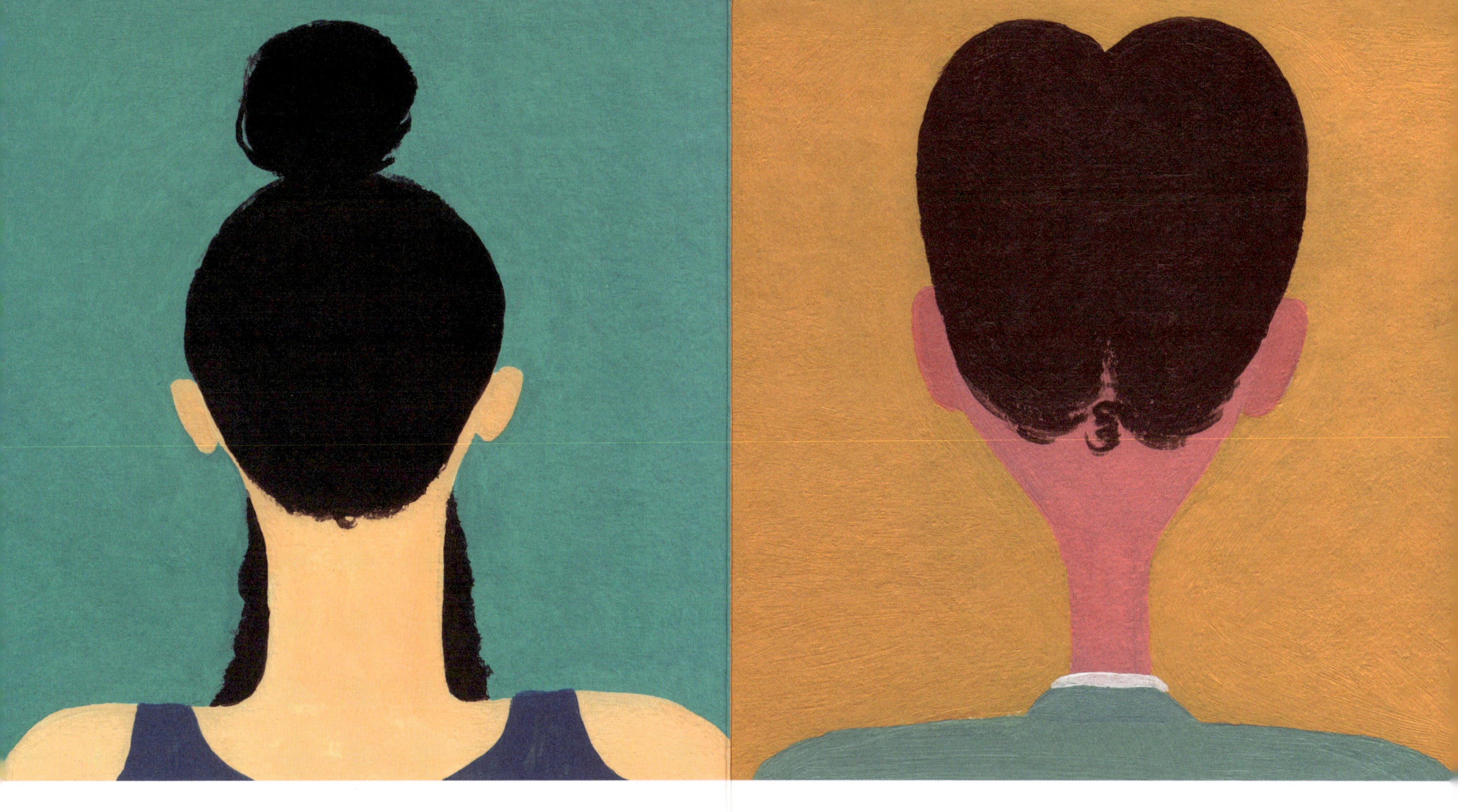

Man Bun (Mun)

Duck's Arse

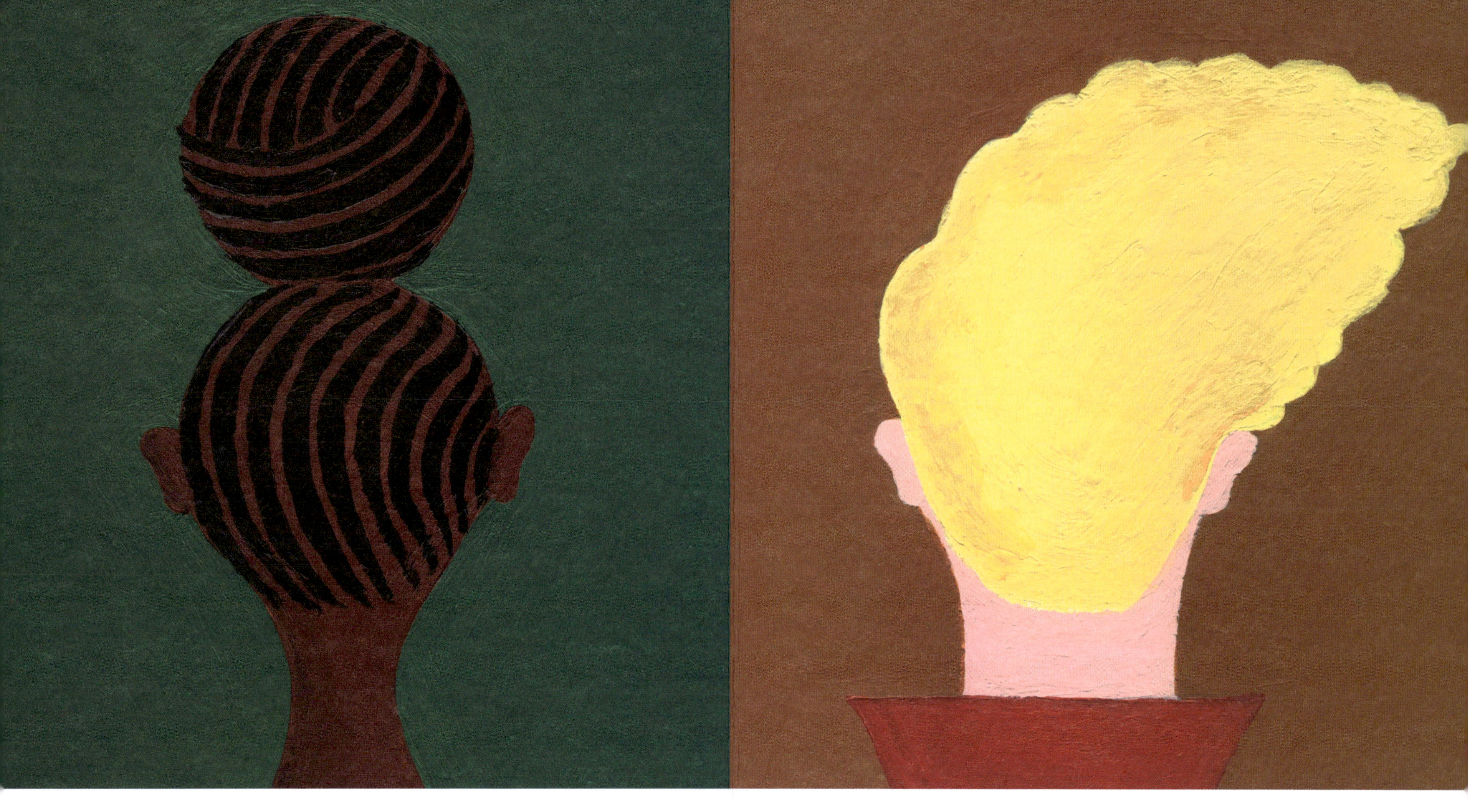

Wool Balls   Scambled Eggs

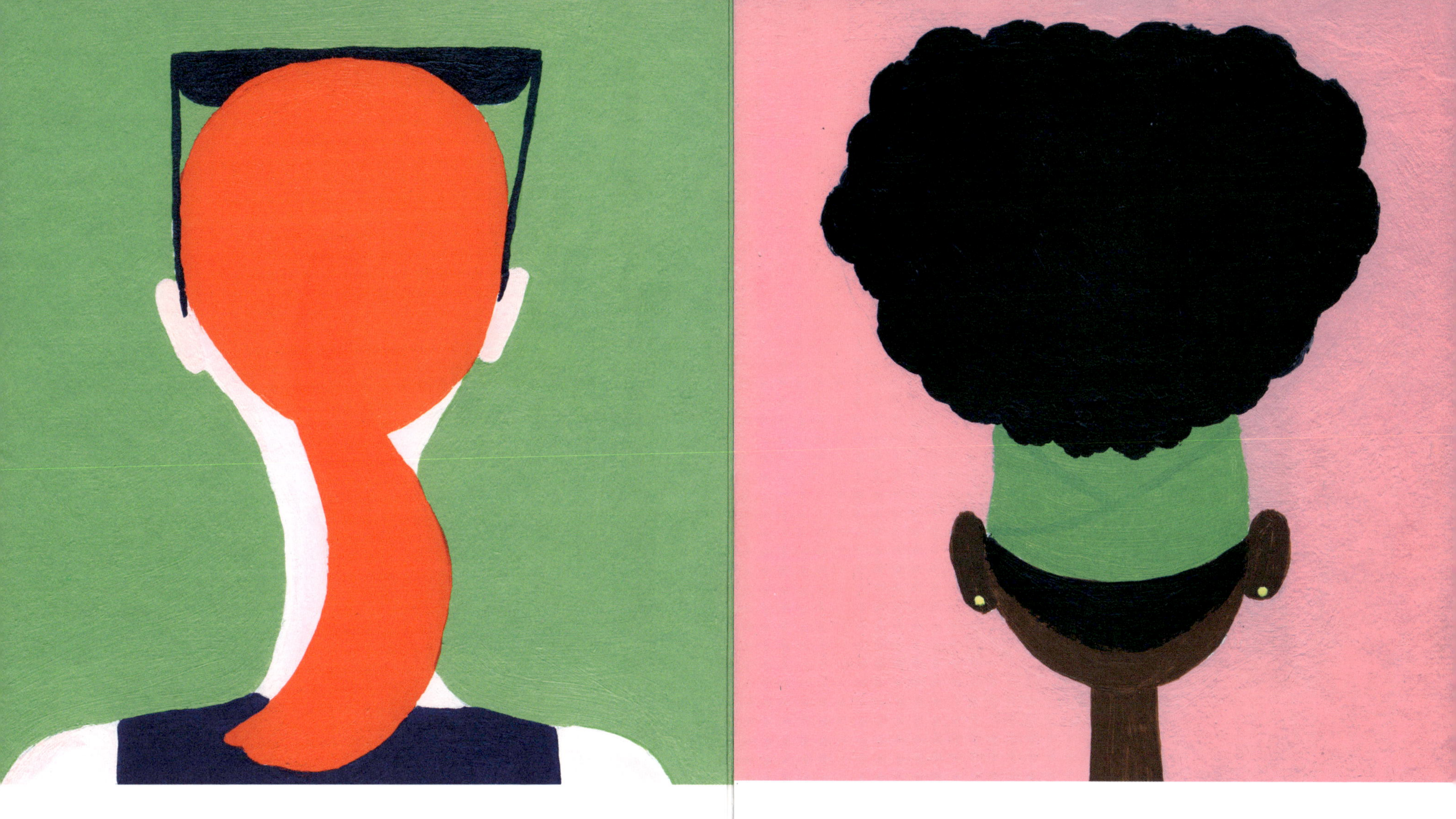

American Tourist

Fro Control

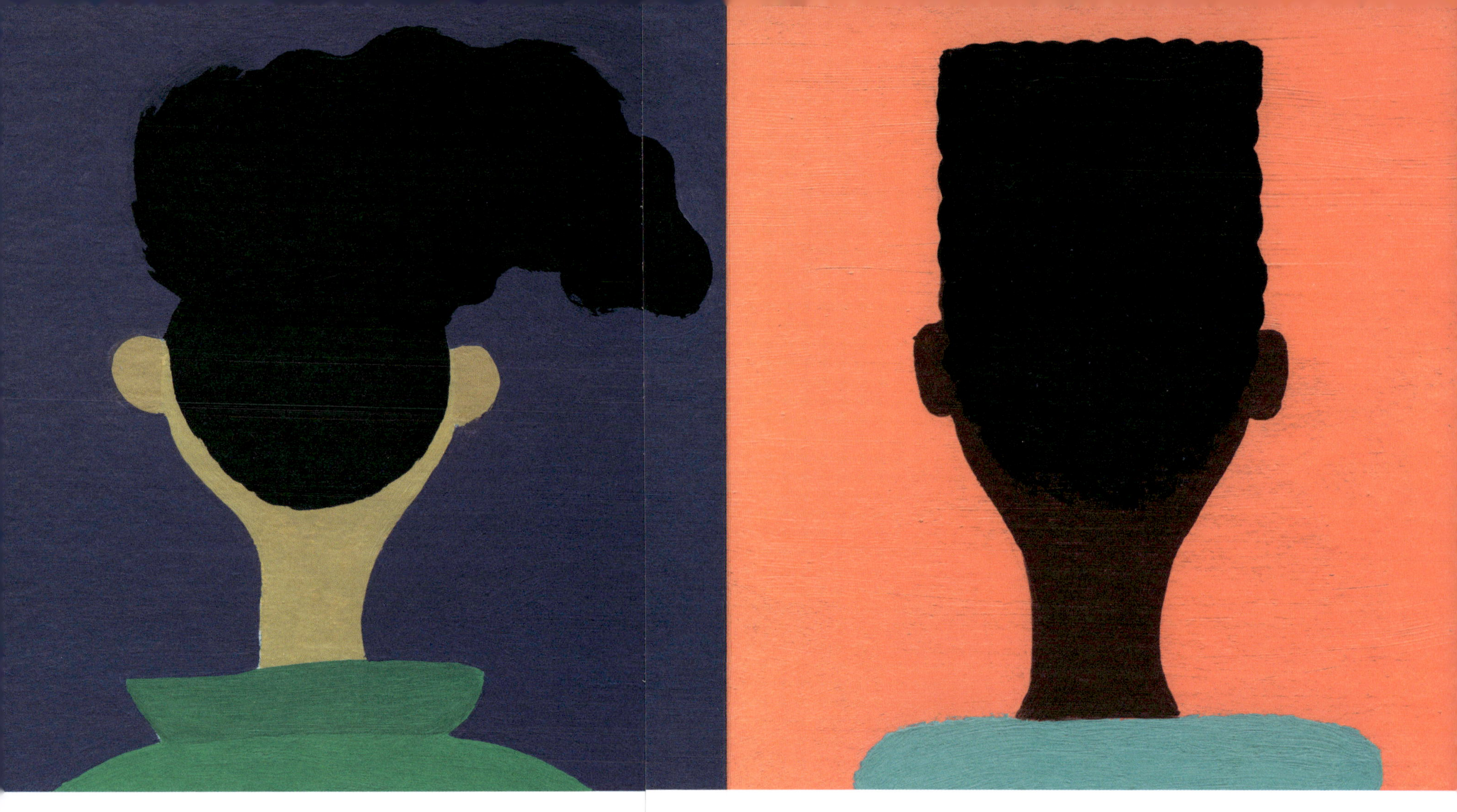

Windsock

Hi-top

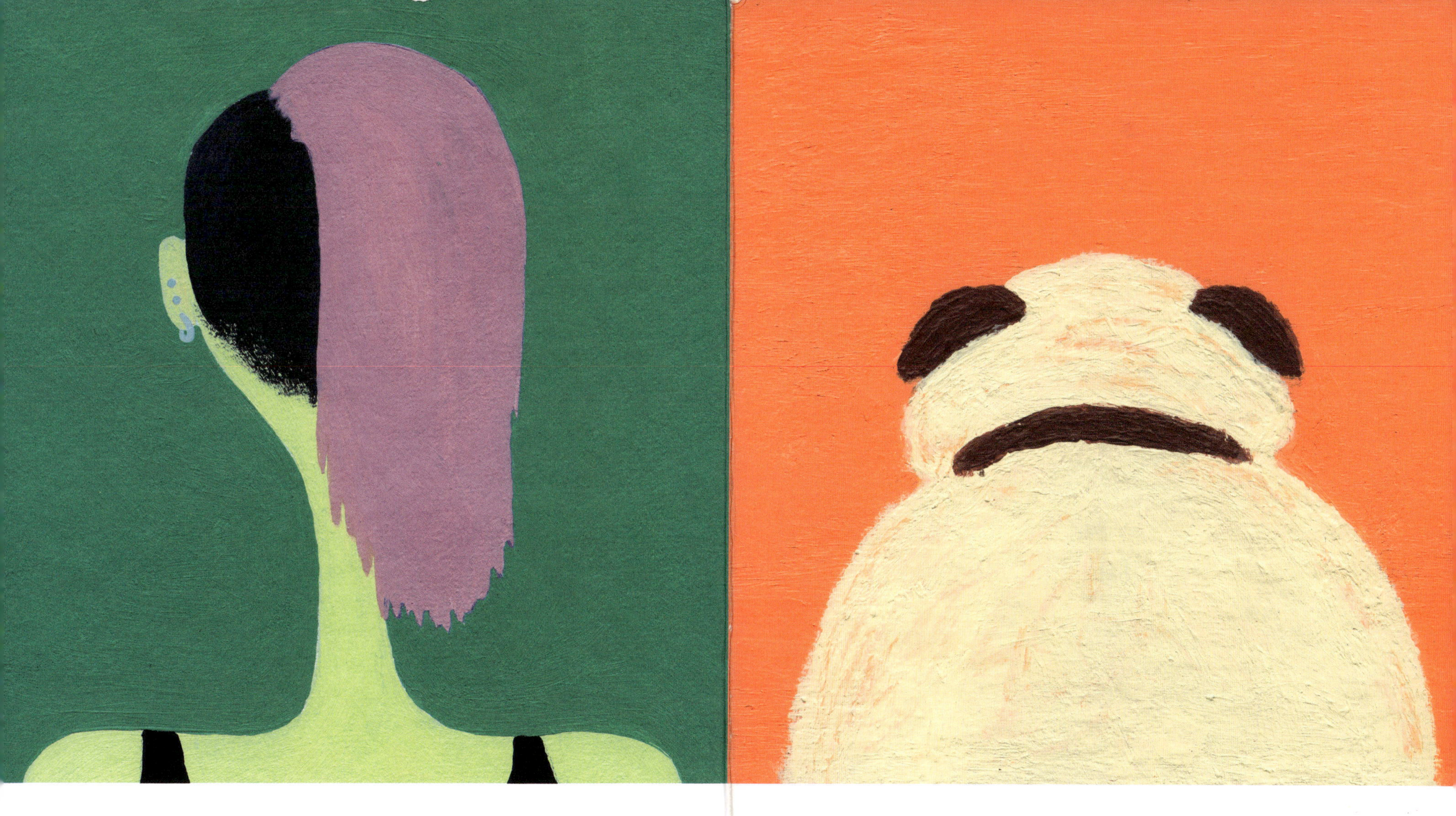

Bit On The Side

Hair Of The Dog

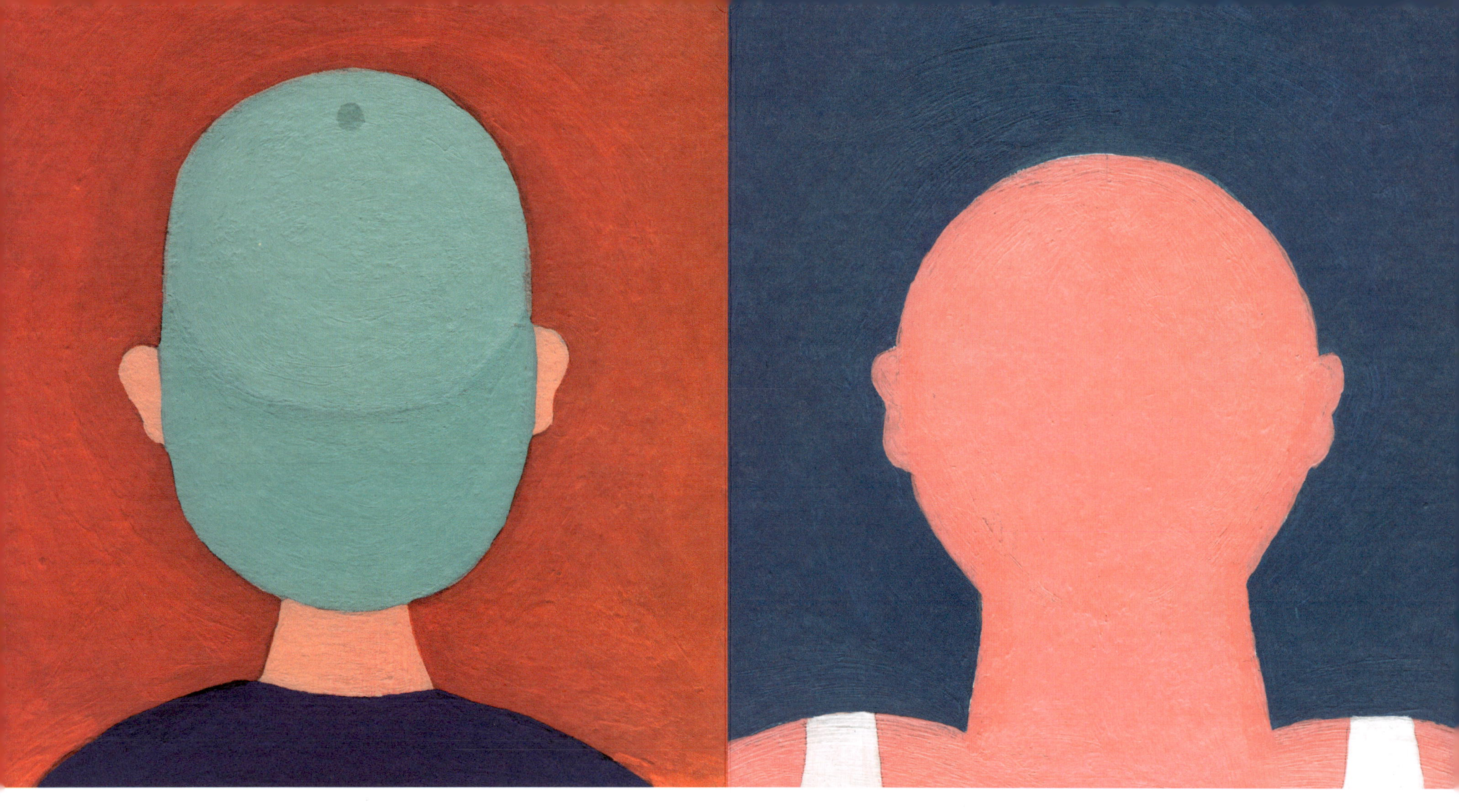

Hoxton Lurker
Bald Brute